FAVORITE TV THEMES – BIG-NOTE PIANO

ISBN 978-1-5400-5305-3

Visit Hal Leonard Online at
www.halleonard.com

Contact us:
Hal Leonard
7777 West Bluemound Road
Milwaukee, WI 53213
Email: info@halleonard.com

In Europe, contact:
Hal Leonard Europe Limited
42 Wigmore Street
Marylebone, London, W1U 2RN
Email: info@halleonardeurope.com

In Australia, contact:
Hal Leonard Australia Pty. Ltd.
4 Lentara Court
Cheltenham, Victoria, 3192 Australia
Email: info@halleonard.com.au

ADDAMS FAMILY THEME

Theme from the TV Show and Movie

Music and Lyrics by
VIC MIZZY

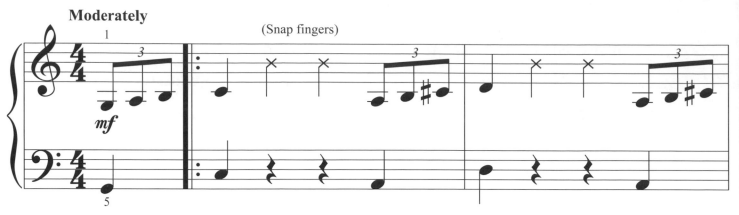

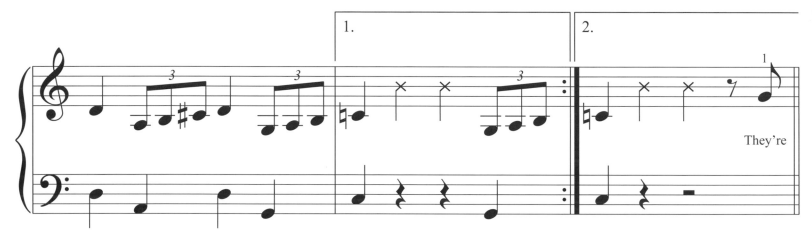

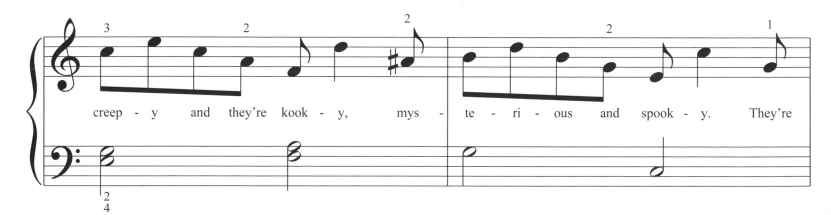

creep-y and they're kook-y, mys-te-ri-ous and spook-y. They're

al-to-geth-er ook-y, the Ad-dams Fam-i-ly. The house is a mu-se-um where

peo - ple come to see 'em. They real - ly are a scree-um, the Ad-dams Fam - i - ly.

Neat. *Sweet.*

Pe - tite! So get a witch -'s shawl on, a broom-stick you can crawl on; we're

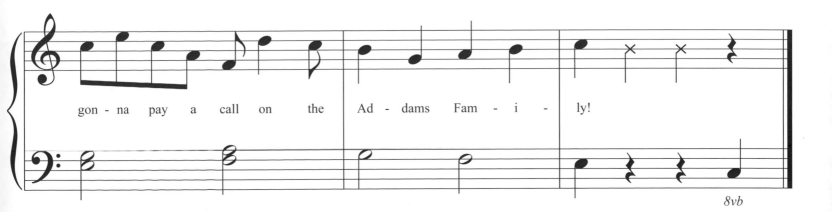

gon - na pay a call on the Ad - dams Fam - i - ly!

8vb

THE BRADY BUNCH
Theme from the Paramount Television Series THE BRADY BUNCH

Words and Music by SHERWOOD SCHWARTZ
and FRANK DEVOL

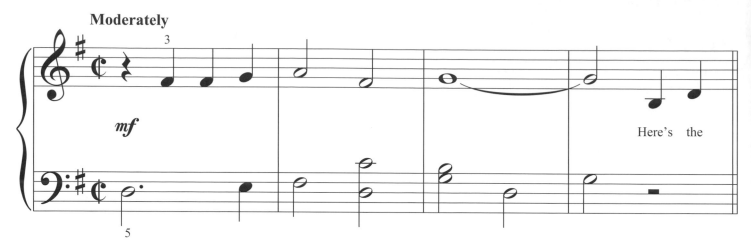

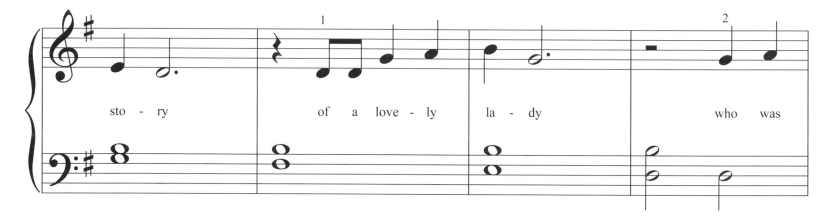

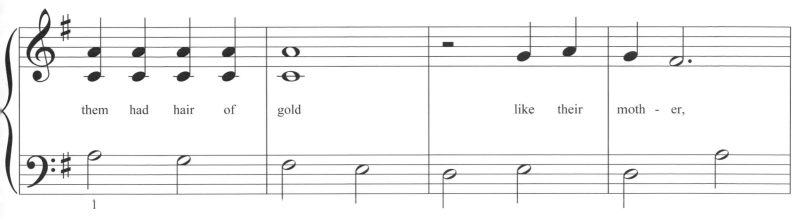

them had hair of gold   like their moth - er,

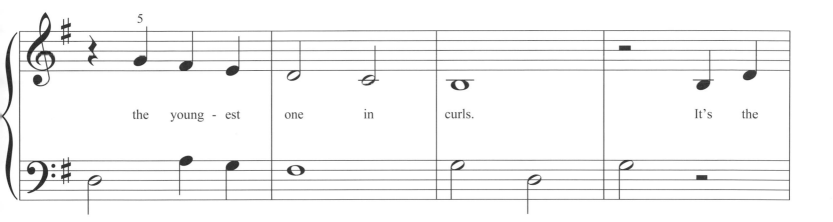

the young - est one in curls.   It's the

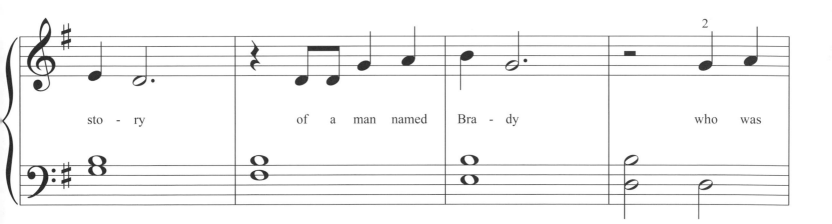

sto - ry of a man named Bra - dy who was

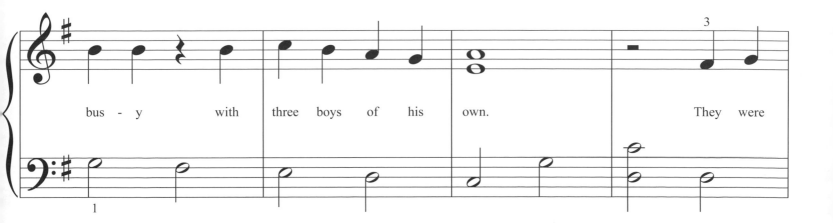

bus - y with three boys of his own.   They were

four men   liv - ing all   to - geth - er,   yet they were

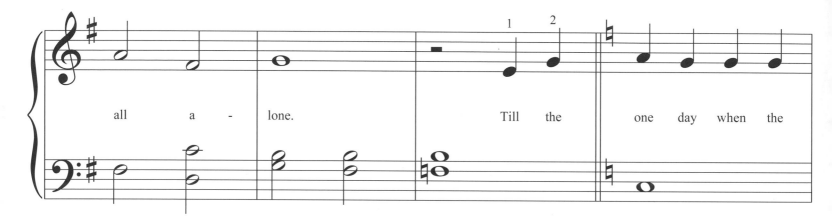

all   a -   lone.   Till the   one day when the

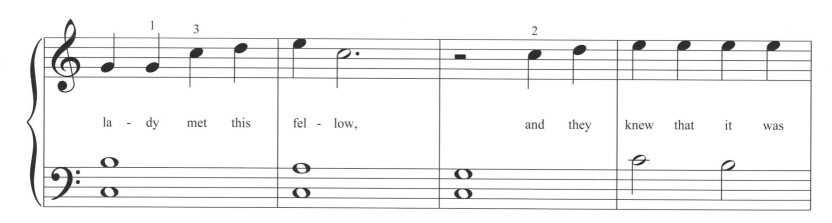

la - dy met this   fel - low,   and they   knew that it was

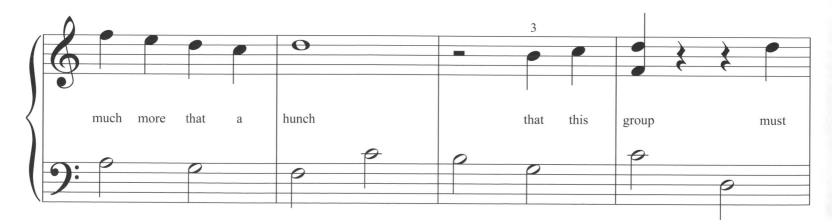

much more that a   hunch   that this   group   must

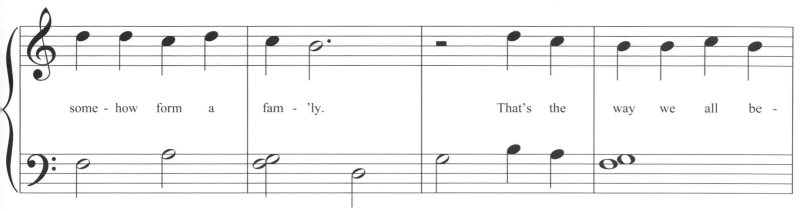

some - how form a fam - 'ly. That's the way we all be -

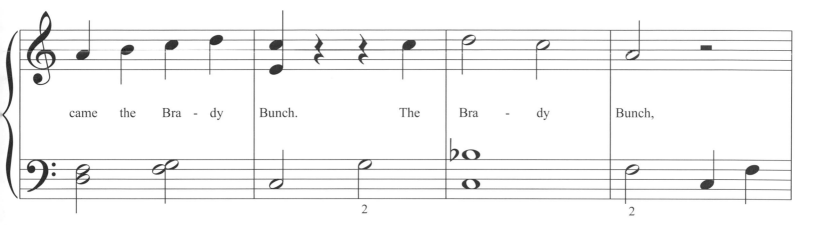

came the Bra - dy Bunch. The Bra - dy Bunch,

the Bra - dy Bunch. That's the way

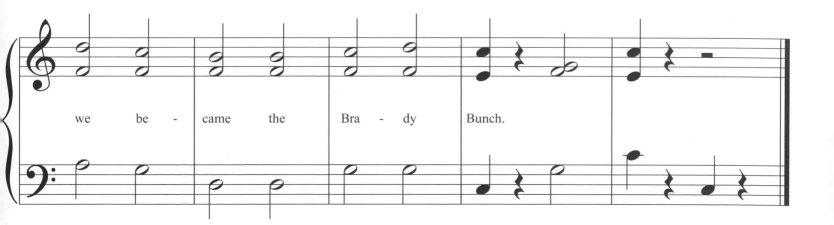

we be - came the Bra - dy Bunch.

CBS SPORTS NFL THEME

By ELLIOT SCHRAEGER
and WALTER LEVINSKY

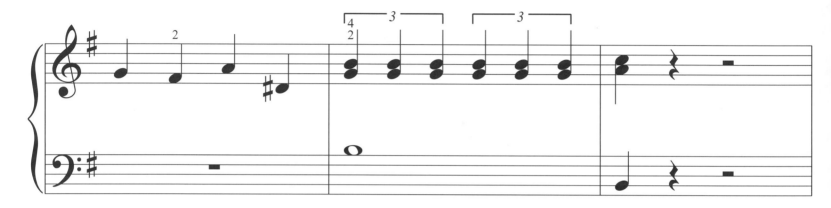

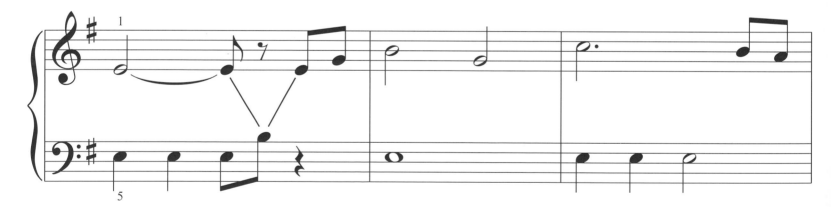

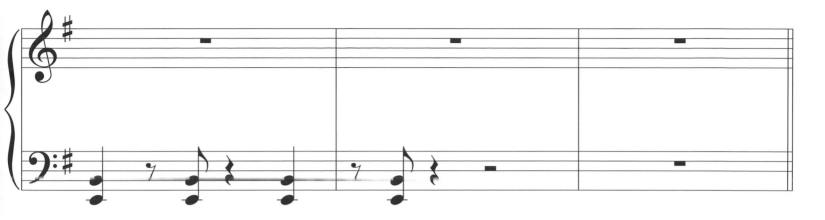

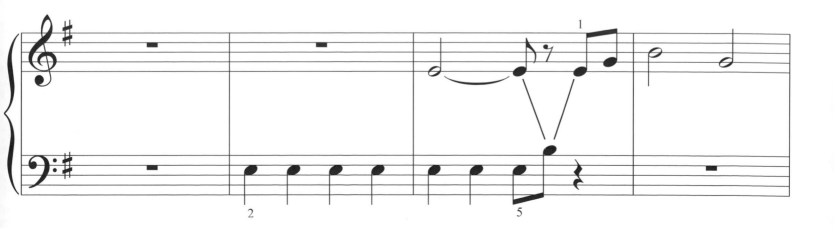

HAPPY DAYS
Theme from the Paramount Television Series HAPPY DAYS

Words by NORMAN GIMBEL
Music by CHARLES FOX

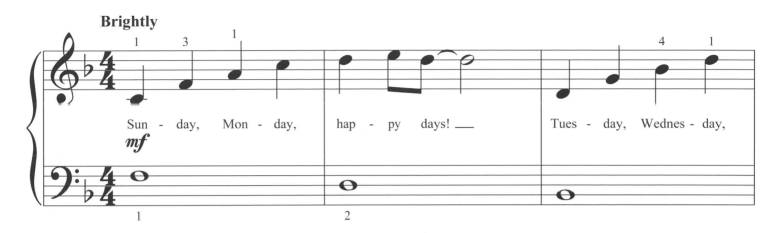

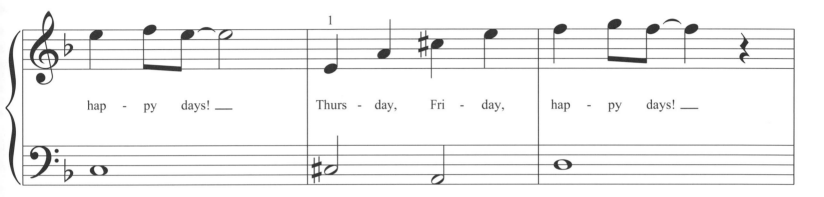

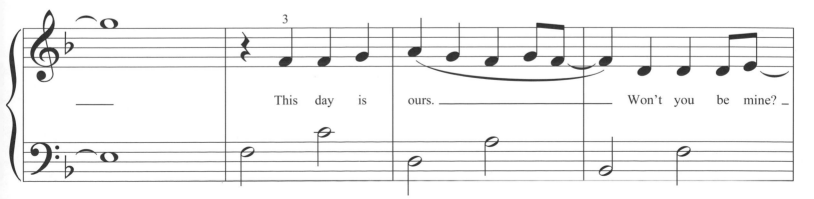

14

This day is ours. _____ Won't you be mine? ____

This day is ours. _____ Oh, please be mine. _

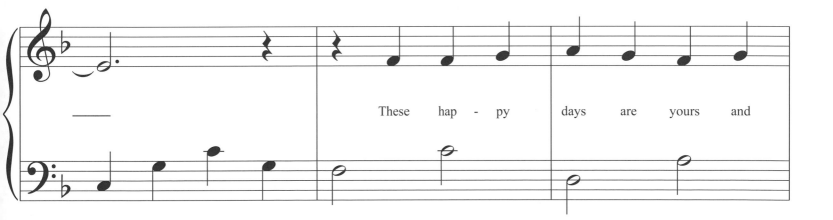

____ These hap - py days are yours and

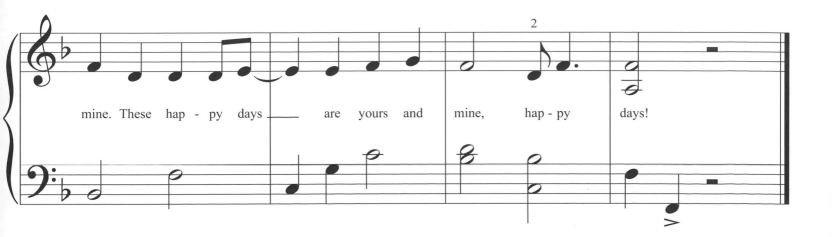

mine. These hap - py days ____ are yours and mine, hap - py days!

EVERYBODY LOVES RAYMOND
(Opening Theme)

Words and Music by TERRY TROTTER
and RICK MAROTTA

Bright easy Jazz

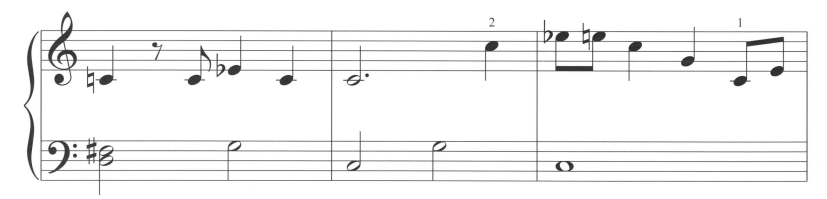

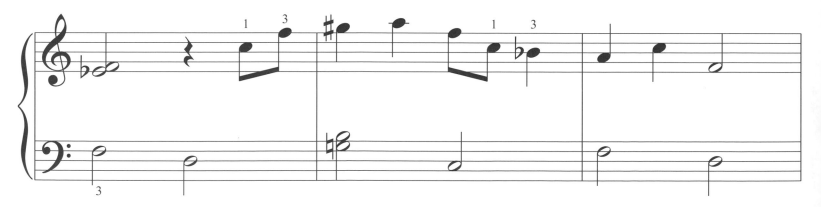

THE GOLDBERGS MAIN TITLE

Music by BRIAN MAZZAFERRI

Moderately fast

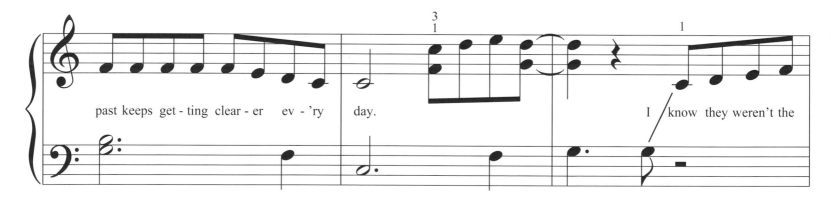

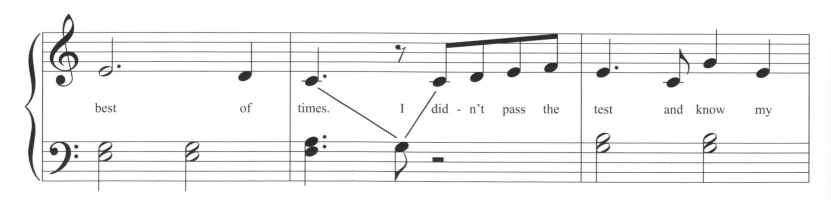

lines. But I would-n't change a thing, 'cause all those things were

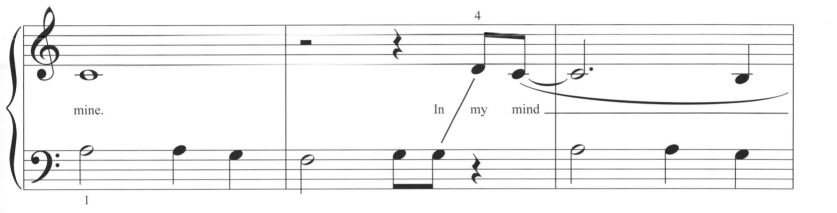

mine.

In my mind

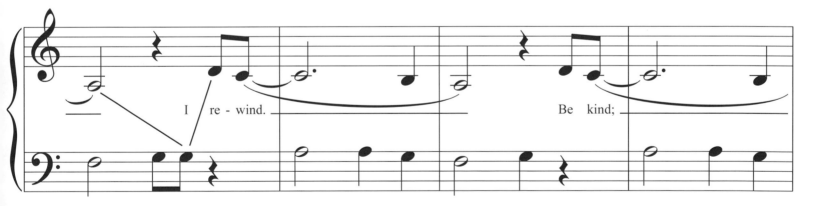

I re - wind.

Be kind;

re - wind.

HAWAII FIVE-O THEME
from the Television Series

By MORT STEVENS

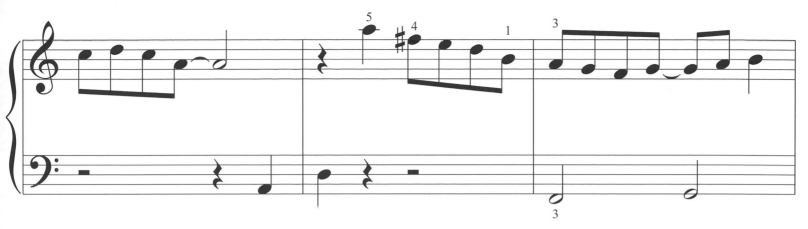

HEY BEAUTIFUL

from HOW I MET YOUR MOTHER

Words and Music by CARTER BAYS
and CRAIG THOMAS

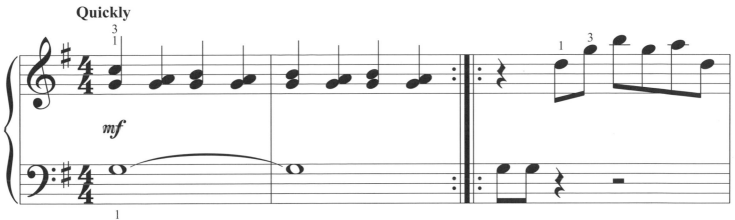

Shed a smoke, bro-ken in, tale of woe oh, oh, com-mis-er-at-in' so

hard to let go. I'm on your back, scratch-in' ear-ly and your can-di-date,

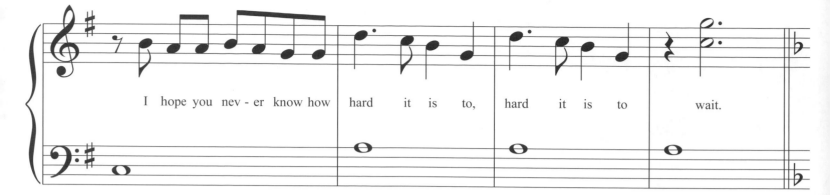

I hope you nev - er know how hard it is to, hard it is to wait.

Hey beau - ti - ful, I seen you com - in'.

Oh, no you don't, walk a - way from me.

Oh, oh, oh, oh, oh, oh, oh, oh, oh, hey, beau - ti - ful.

Oh, oh, oh, oh, oh, oh, oh, oh, oh, hey, beau - ti -

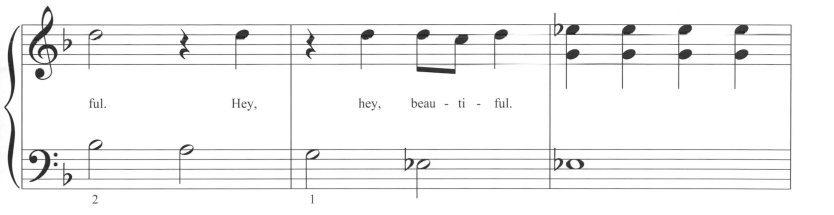

ful. Hey, hey, beau - ti - ful.

Pa pa pa pa pa pa pa

Play 4 times

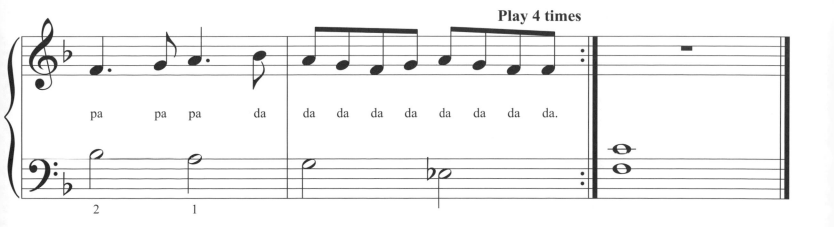

pa pa pa da da da da da da da da da.

I LOVE LUCY
from the Television Series

Lyric by HAROLD ADAMSON
Music by ELIOT DANIEL

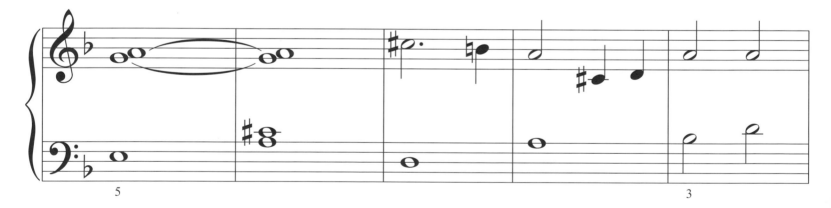

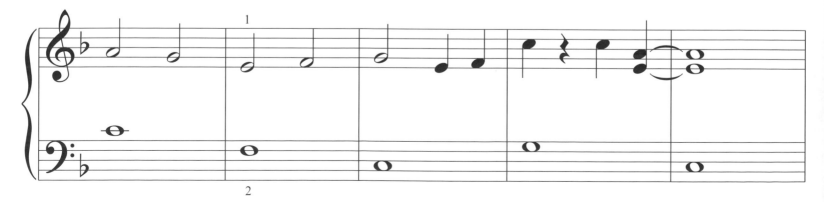

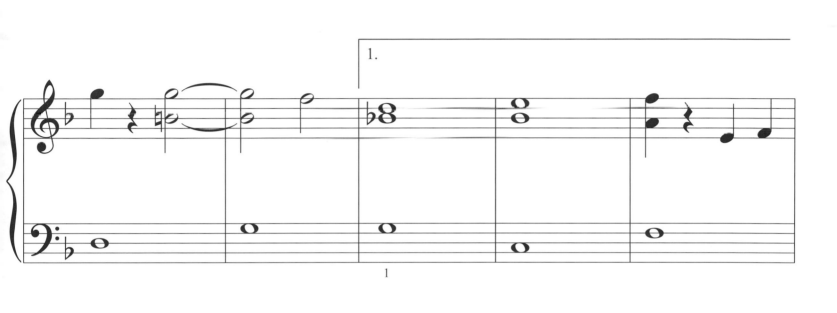

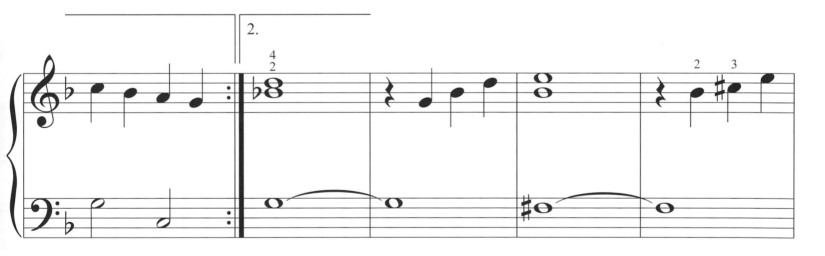

JEOPARDY THEME

Music by MERV GRIFFIN

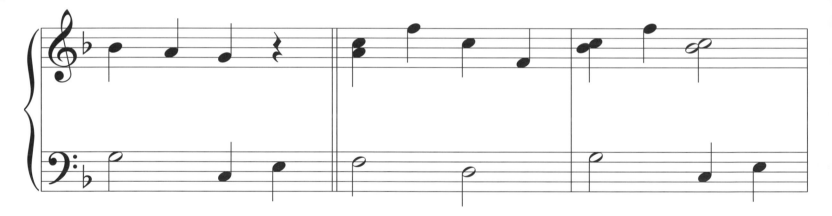

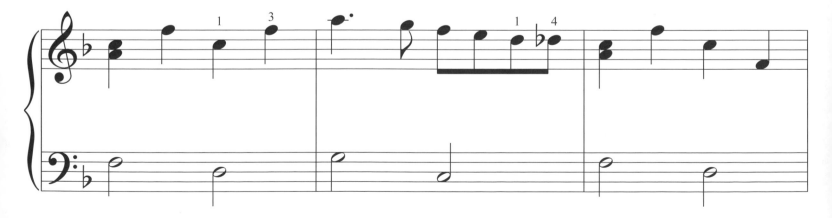

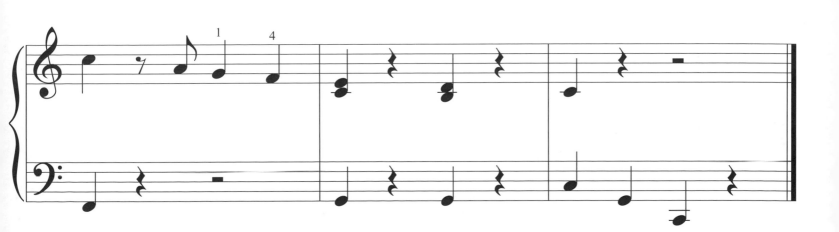

MISSION: IMPOSSIBLE THEME

from the Paramount Television Series MISSION: IMPOSSIBLE

By LALO SCHIFRIN

Moderately, with drive

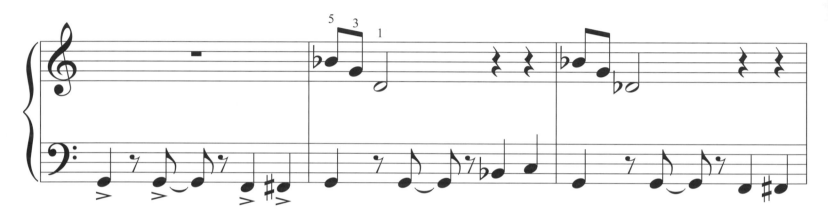

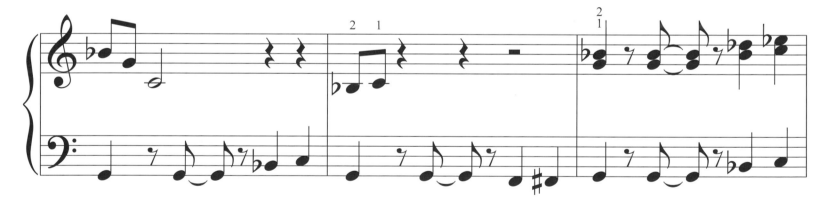

THE MUPPET SHOW THEME
from the Television Series

Words and Music by JIM HENSON
and SAM POTTLE

It's time to play the mu - sic.
It's time to put on make - up.
It's time to

light the lights. ___
dress up right. ___
It's time to meet the Mup - pets on The
It's time to raise the cur - tain on The

1.
Mup - pet Show ___ to - night.

2.
Mup - pet Show ___ to - night.

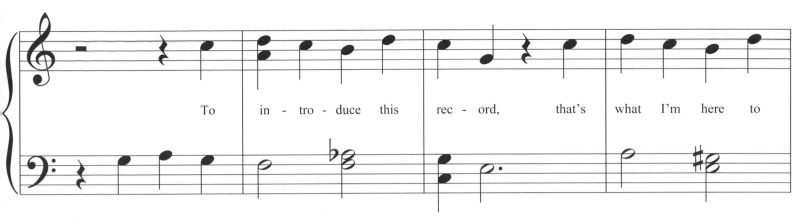

To in - tro - duce this rec - ord, that's what I'm here to

do. So it real - ly makes me hap - py to

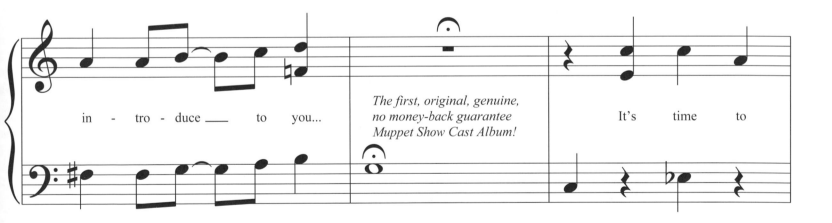

in - tro - duce ___ to you...

The first, original, genuine, no money-back guarantee Muppet Show Cast Album!

It's time to

put on make - up. It's time to dress up right. ___

It's time to get things start - ed on the most sen - sa - tion - al,

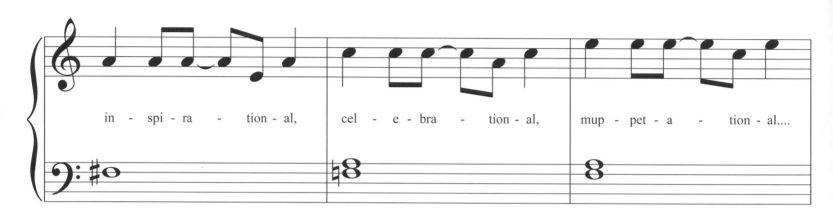

in - spi - ra - tion - al, cel - e - bra - tion - al, mup - pet - a - tion - al....

This is what we call The Mup - pet

Show!

NFL ON FOX THEME

from the Fox Sports Broadcasts of THE NFL ON FOX

By PHIL GARROD,
REED HAYS and SCOTT SCHREER

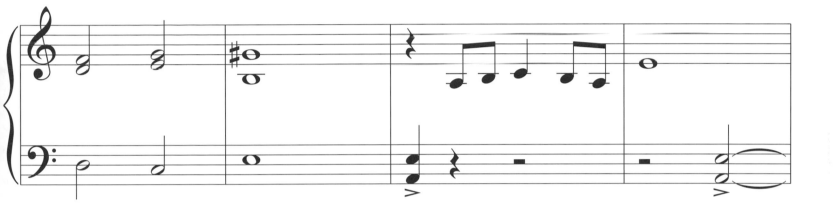

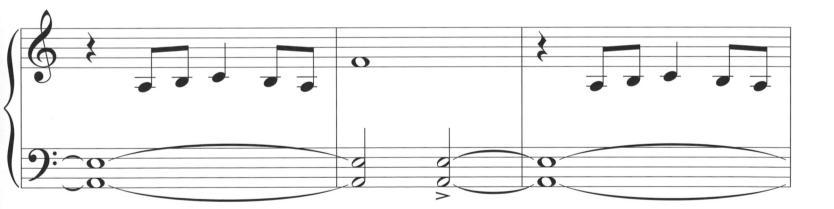

THE PRICE IS RIGHT – OPENING THEME

By EDWARD KALEHOFF

To Coda $\oplus$

D.S. al Coda

CODA

THE OFFICE – THEME

from THE OFFICE

By JAY FERGUSON

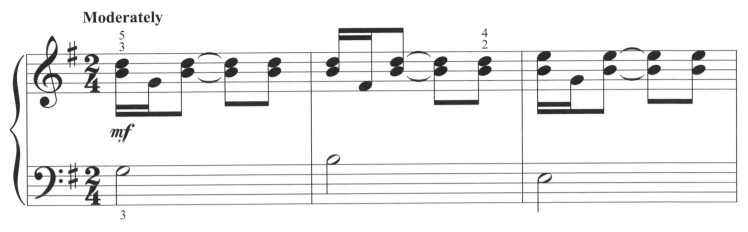

PARKS AND RECREATION THEME

Words and Music by GABY MORENO
and VINCENT JONES

Moderately fast

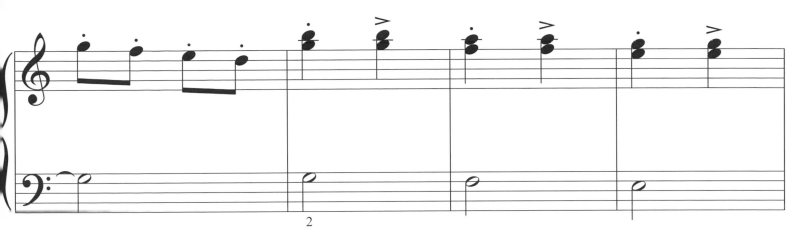

SESAME STREET THEME

from the Television Series SESAME STREET

Words by BRUCE HART,
JON STONE and JOE RAPOSO
Music by JOE RAPOSO

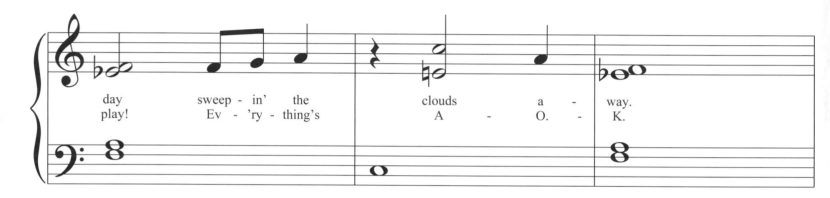

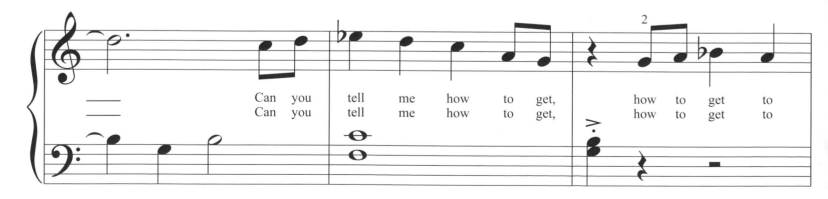

THEME FROM THE SIMPSONS™

from the Twentieth Century Fox Television Series THE SIMPSONS

Music by DANNY ELFMAN

Moderately fast, in 2

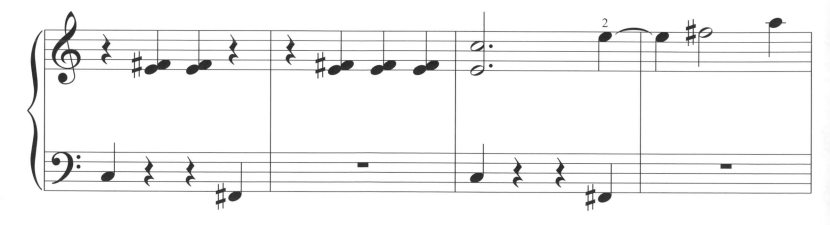

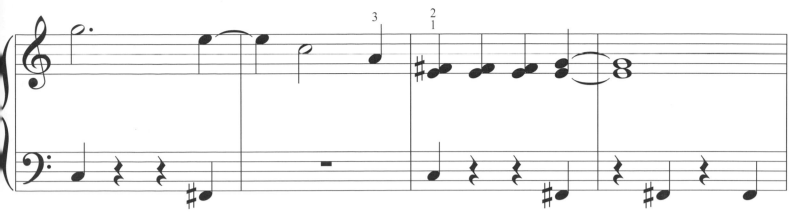

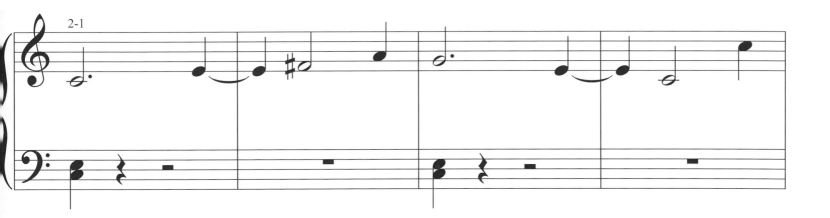

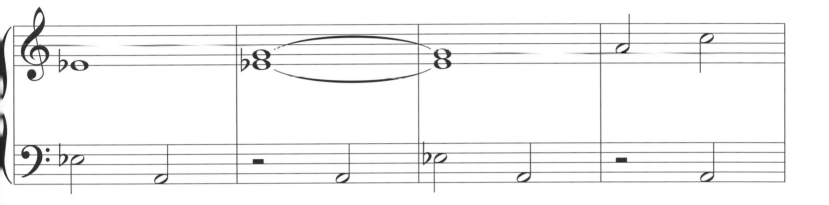

THEME FROM "STAR TREK®"

from the Paramount Television Series STAR TREK

Words by GENE RODDENBERRY
Music by ALEXANDER COURAGE

Moderately

Be - yond ___ the rim of the star - light, ___

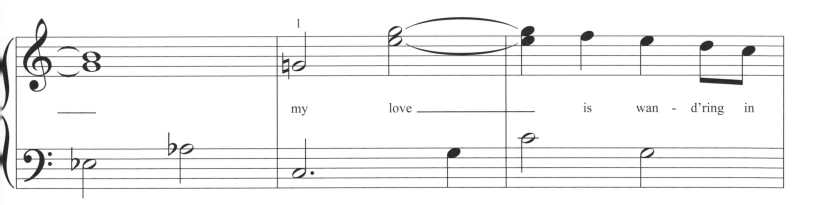

___ my love ___ is wan - d'ring in

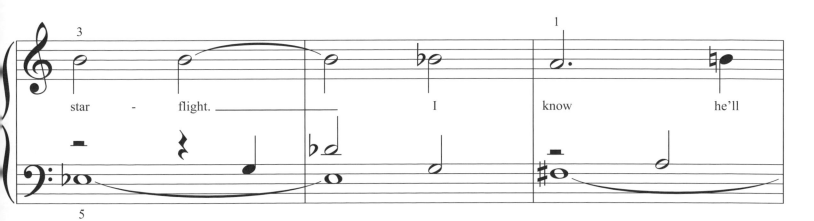

star - flight. ___ I know he'll

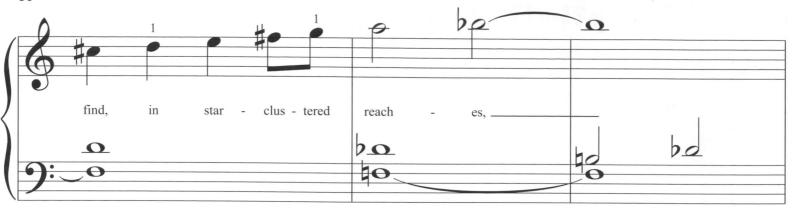

find, in star - clus - tered reach - es, _____

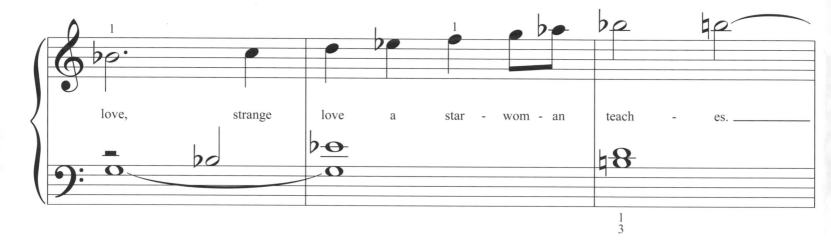

love, strange love a star - wom - an teach - es. _____

1
3

_____ I know _____ his jour - ney ends

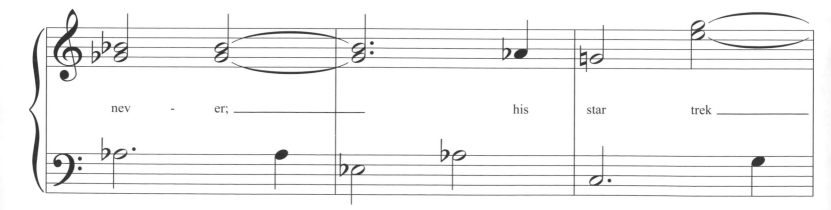

nev - er; _____ his star trek _____

_____ will go on for - ev - er. _____ But tell him

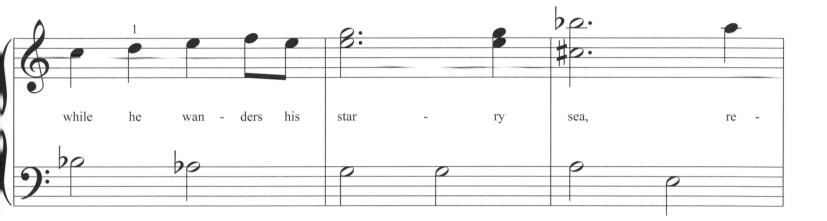

while he wan - ders his star - ry sea, re -

mem - ber, _____ re - mem - ber me. _____

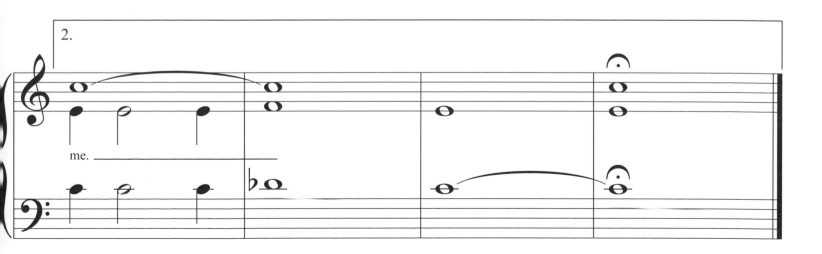

me. _____

SPONGEBOB SQUAREPANTS THEME SONG

from SPONGEBOB SQUAREPANTS

Words and Music by MARK HARRISON,
BLAISE SMITH, STEVE HILLENBURG
and DEREK DRYMON

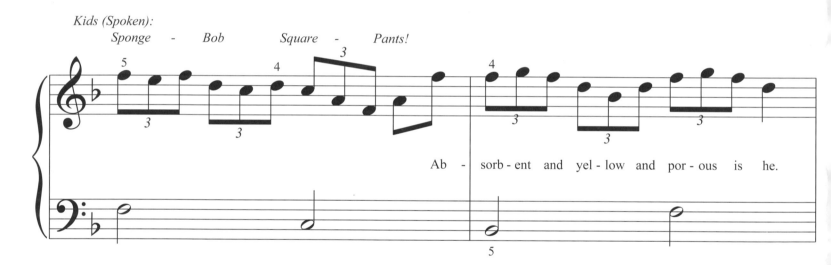

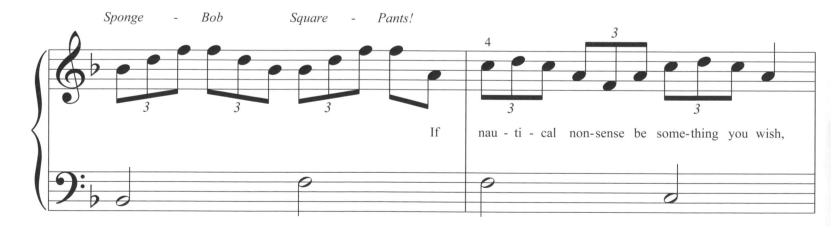

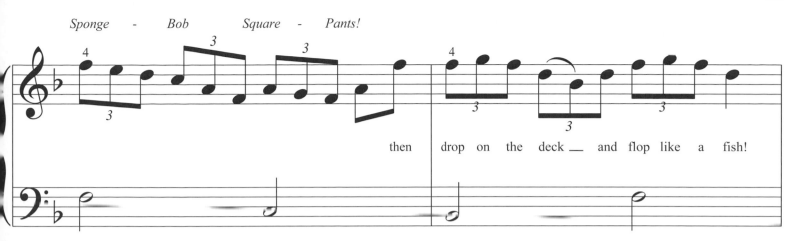

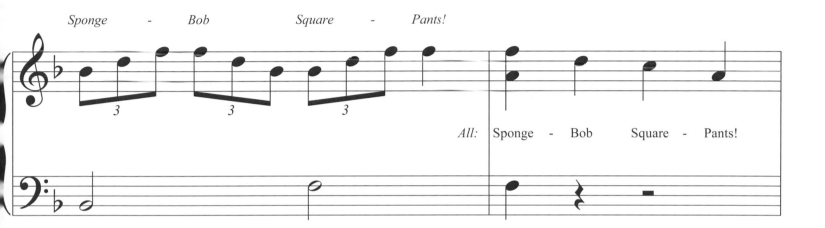

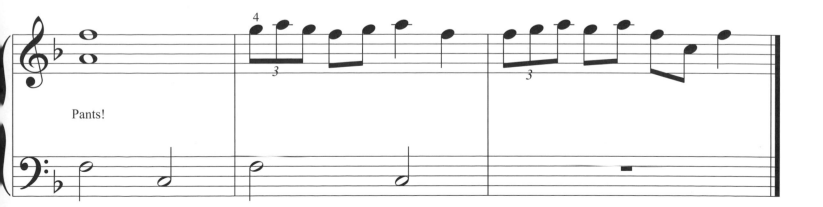

THE WALKING DEAD – MAIN TITLE

from THE WALKING DEAD

By BEAR McCREARY
and STEVEN KAPLAN

Moderately fast, in 2

WON'T YOU BE MY NEIGHBOR?

(It's a Beautiful Day in the Neighborhood)
from MISTER ROGERS' NEIGHBORHOOD

Words and Music by
FRED ROGERS

al - ways want-ed to live in a neigh-bor - hood with you, _____ so

let's make the most of this beau-ti-ful day. Since we're to-geth-er, we might as well say:

To Coda ⊕

Would you be mine? Could you be mine? Won't you be my neigh-bor? Won't you please, won't you please?

D.C. al Coda
(with repeat)

Please won't you be my neigh-bor?

CODA
⊕

Please won't you be my neigh-bor?

Big Fun with Big-Note Piano Books!

These songbooks feature exciting easy arrangements for beginning piano students.

Best of Adele

Now even beginners can play their favorite Adele tunes! This book features big-note arrangements of 10 top songs: Chasing Pavements • Daydreamer • Hometown Glory • Lovesong • Make You Feel My Love • One and Only • Rolling in the Deep • Set Fire to the Rain • Someone like You • Turning Tables.
00308601 ....$14.99

Beatles' Best

27 classics for beginners to enjoy, including: Can't Buy Me Love • Eleanor Rigby • Hey Jude • Michelle • Here, There and Everywhere • When I'm Sixty-Four • Yesterday • and more.
00222561......................................$14.99

The Best Songs Ever

70 favorites, featuring: Body and Soul • Crazy • Edelweiss • Fly Me to the Moon • Georgia on My Mind • Imagine • The Lady Is a Tramp • Memory • A String of Pearls • Tears in Heaven • Unforgettable • You Are So Beautiful • and more.
00310425 ....$19.95

Children's Favorite Movie Songs

arranged by Phillip Keveren
16 favorites from films, including: The Bare Necessities • Beauty and the Beast • Can You Feel the Love Tonight • Do-Re-Mi • The Rainbow Connection • Tomorrow • Zip-A-Dee-Doo-Dah • and more.
00310838 ....$12.99

Classical Music's Greatest Hits

24 beloved classical pieces, including: Air on the G String • Ave Maria • By the Beautiful Blue Danube • Canon in D • Eine Kleine Nachtmusik • Für Elise • Ode to Joy • Romeo and Juliet • Waltz of the Flowers • more.
00310475 ....$12.99

Disney Big-Note Collection

Over 40 Disney favorites, including: Circle of Life • Colors of the Wind • Hakuna Matata • It's a Small World • Under the Sea • A Whole New World • Winnie the Pooh • Zip-A-Dee-Doo-Dah • and more.
00316056..$19.99

Essential Classical

22 simplified piano pieces from top composers, including: Ave Maria (Schubert) • Blue Danube Waltz (Strauss) • Für Elise (Beethoven) • Jesu, Joy of Man's Desiring (Bach) • Morning (Grieg) • Pomp and Circumstance (Elgar) • and many more.
00311205......................................$10.99

Favorite Children's Songs

arranged by Bill Boyd
29 easy arrangements of songs to play and sing with children: Peter Cottontail • I Whistle a Happy Tune • It's a Small World • On the Good Ship Lollipop • The Rainbow Connection • and more!
00240251 ....$12.99

Frozen

9 songs from this hit Disney film, plus full-color illustrations from the movie. Songs include the standout single "Let It Go", plus: Do You Want to Build a Snowman? • For the First Time in Forever • Reindeer(s) Are Better Than People • and more.
00126105 ....$12.99

Happy Birthday to You and Other Great Songs for Big-Note Piano

16 essential favorites, including: Chitty Chitty Bang Bang • Good Night • Happy Birthday to You • Heart and Soul • Over the Rainbow • Sing • This Land Is Your Land • and more.
00119636 ....$9.99

Elton John – Greatest Hits

20 of his biggest hits, including: Bennie and the Jets • Candle in the Wind • Crocodile Rock • Rocket Man • Tiny Dancer • Your Song • and more.
00221832......................................$14.99

Les Misérables

14 favorites from the Broadway sensation arranged for beginning pianists. Titles include: At the End of the Day • Bring Him Home • Castle on a Cloud • I Dreamed a Dream • In My Life • On My Own • Who Am I? • and more.
00221812 ....$15.99

The Phantom of the Opera

9 songs from the Broadway spectacular, including: All I Ask of You • Angel of Music • Masquerade • The Music of the Night • The Phantom of the Opera • The Point of No Return • Prima Donna • Think of Me • Wishing You Were Somehow Here Again.
00110006 ....$14.99

Pride & Prejudice
Music from the Motion Picture Soundtrack

12 piano pieces from the 2006 Oscar-nominated film: Another Dance • Darcy's Letter • Georgiana • Leaving Netherfield • Liz on Top of the World • Meryton Townhall • The Secret Life of Daydreams • Stars and Butterflies • and more.
00316125 ....$12.99

The Sound of Music

arranged by Phillip Keveren
9 favorites: Climb Ev'ry Mountain • Do-Re-Mi • Edelweiss • The Lonely Goatherd • Maria • My Favorite Things • Sixteen Going on Seventeen • So Long, Farewell • The Sound of Music.
00316057......................................$10.99

Best of Taylor Swift

A dozen top tunes from this crossover sensation: Fearless • Fifteen • Hey Stephen • Love Story • Our Song • Picture to Burn • Teardrops on My Guitar • White Horse • You Belong with Me • and more.
00307143 ....$12.99

Worship Favorites

20 powerful songs: Above All • Come, Now Is the Time to Worship • I Could Sing of Your Love Forever • More Precious Than Silver • Open the Eyes of My Heart • Shout to the Lord • and more.
00311207..$12.99

Complete song lists online at
www.halleonard.com

0719
060